Pebble® Plus

BIG

BIG PREDATORS

by Catherine Ipcizade

Consulting Editor: Gail Saunders-Smith, PhD

Consultant: Deborah Nuzzolo
Education Manager
SeaWorld, San Diego

Capstone press®

Mankato, Minnesota

Pebble Plus is published by Capstone Press,
151 Good Counsel Drive, P.O. Box 669, Mankato, Minnesota 56002.
www.capstonepress.com

Books published by Capstone Press are manufactured with paper
containing at least 10 percent post-consumer waste.

Library of Congress Cataloging-in-Publication Data
Ipcizade, Catherine.
Big predators / By Catherine Ipcizade.
p. cm. — (Pebble plus. Big)
Summary: "Simple text and photographs feature big predators" — Provided by publisher.
Includes bibliographical references and index.
ISBN 978-1-4296-3316-1 (library binding)
1. Predatory animals — Juvenile literature. I. Title. II. Series.
QL758.I63 2010
591.5'3 — dc22   2009001615

Editorial Credits
Erika L. Shores, editor; Ted Williams, designer; Jo Miller, media researcher

Photo Credits
iStockphoto/Mark Wilson, 11
Minden Pictures/Suzi Eszterhas, 21
Peter Arnold/Biosphoto/Born Olivier, cover; Biosphoto/Bruemmer Fred, 15; Biosphoto/Heuclin Daniel, 9;
  Biosphoto/Vernay Pierre, 5
Photo Researchers Inc/Martin Wendler, 13
Seapics/C & M Fallows, 17
Shutterstock/Christos Georghiou, cover (background); Evlakhov Valeriy, 19; FloridaStock, 7; javarman, cover
  (background); MTrebbin, cover (background); Vladimir Korostyshevskiy, 1

Note to Parents and Teachers

The Big series supports national science standards related to life science. This book describes
and illustrates big predators. The images support early readers in understanding the text. The
repetition of words and phrases helps early readers learn new words. This book also introduces
early readers to subject-specific vocabulary words, which are defined in the Glossary section.
Early readers may need assistance to read some words and to use the Table of Contents,
Glossary, Read More, Internet Sites, and Index sections of the book.

Table of Contents

Big

Leap! Swoop! Chomp!
Big predators catch prey
in all kinds of ways.

Tigers can be up to 11 feet
(3.4 meters) long, from
head to tail.

Eagles swoop down
from the sky.
Their big talons
grab fish from the water.

Size:

7-foot (2.1-meter) wingspan

Tarantulas use eight big legs
to leap on prey.
Then the spiders sting
with a deadly bite.

Size:
up to 12-inch
(30-centimeter) leg span

Bigger

Female lions hunt
on the savanna.
Their big eyes
easily spot wildebeests.

Size:
up to 11.5 feet (3.5 meters) long,
from head to tail

Anacondas grab prey
with a big bite.
Then they squeeze
the animal to death.

Size:

up to 20 feet (6 meters) long

Biggest

Polar bears wait for
a seal to come close.
Big bear paws attack.

Size:
up to 9.8 feet (3 meters) long

Great white sharks zoom through the ocean. Their big jaws slice through prey.

Size:

up to 20 feet (6 meters) long

Crocodiles lie in wait
with 68 big teeth.
Snap! They grab their meal.

Size:
up to 23 feet (7 meters) long

Killer whales make clicking sounds as they circle prey. These big predators work together to catch food.

Size:
up to 28 feet (8.5 meters) long

Glossary

predator — an animal that hunts other animals for food

prey — an animal hunted by another animal for food

savanna — a flat, grassy area of land with few or no trees

sting — to hurt with a poisoned tip

talon — an eagle's claw; a talon has four toes, each with a very sharp curved nail.

wildebeest — a large African animal with a head like an ox, two curved horns, and a long tail

Read More

Eckart, Edana. *Tarantula.* Animals of the World. New York: Children's Press, 2005.

Francis, Suzanne. *On the Prowl: Animal Hunters.* 3-D Animals in Action. New York: Scholastic, 2007.

Stout, Frankie. *Nature's Nastiest Biters.* Extreme Animals. New York: PowerKids Press, 2008.

Internet Sites

FactHound offers a safe, fun way to find Internet sites related to this book. All of the sites on FactHound have been researched by our staff.

Here's all you do:

Visit *www.facthound.com*

FactHound will fetch the best sites for you!

Index

Word Count: 125
Grade: 1
Early-Intervention Level: 14